631 WILLSON, R.B.

Sporty witch

This book is due for return on or before the last date shown above but it may be renewed by personal application, post, or telephone, quoting this date and details of the book.

Northamptonshire Leisure and Libraries

00 300 285 631

Sporty Witch

By the same author in Hopscotch books:

SECRET WITCH
HOLIDAY WITCH
HUNGRY WITCH

Sporty Witch

Robina Beckles Willson

Illustrated by Azalea Sturdy

HODDER AND STOUGHTON
LONDON SYDNEY AUCKLAND TORONTO

British Library Cataloguing in Publication Data
Willson, Robina Beckles
 Sporty witch. – (Hopscotch)
 I. Title   II. Sturdy, Azalea
 823'.914[J]   PZ7

ISBN 0-340-38890-0

Text copyright © Robina Beckles Willson 1986
Illustrations copyright © Azalea Sturdy 1986

First published 1986

All rights reserved. No part of this publication may be reproduced or transmitted in any form or by any means, electronic or mechanical, including photocopy, recording, or any information storage and retrieval system, without permission in writing from the publisher.

Published by Hodder and Stoughton Children's Books,
a division of Hodder and Stoughton Ltd,
Mill Road, Dunton Green, Sevenoaks, Kent TN13 2YJ

Photoset by Rowland Phototypesetting Ltd,
Bury St Edmunds, Suffolk

Printed in Great Britain by St Edmundsbury Press Ltd,
Bury St Edmunds, Suffolk

'There's an Open Day and Sports at my old school this Saturday,' said Witch. 'So I thought you would like to take me there in your car, Mr Mib.'

'It's quite enough having you, your Cat and your Toad living here, without taking you out at the weekend, when I can have a rest from being caretaker.'

'But the Sports will be a lovely treat for you. Much more fun than work in this office building. We can all go out and see where I was at school when I was a little girl. I've asked Cosy too.'

'Another witch as well;' Mr Mib groaned.

'Don't you remember, she was at school with me, and always a very good girl.'

'Not like you!'

'I was very clever, making up my first magic spells, of course,' Witch told him. 'We could set off early and let you see the school.'

'But my car is so old. It might break down on the way,' Mr Mib protested.

'As if Cat and I, with our magic, would let your car break down,' said Witch scornfully.

Mr Mib made one last try: 'Why don't you go by broomstick? Much more exciting.'

'No, because I want you to come with me,' said Witch. 'So that's all arranged. Call for us at ten o'clock. Cosy has a holiday from her cooking job. She'll meet us here. And I hope she'll bring a picnic.'

'So do I,' said Mr Mib. He felt sure that going back to school with Witch would bring nothing but trouble.

Mr Mib did not know that Witch was training for the school Sports. Every night, when he went home after clearing up the building, she had the place to herself. And she didn't whizz up and down in the lift any more. Nor did she slide down the banisters with Cat and Toad.

Witch did running up and down stairs. She touched her toes, keeping her knees almost straight. She ran races with Cat

and Toad down the corridors in the building. And she tried high jumps over parcel strings they held for her.

'I'm getting fitter every day,' said Witch to Cat. 'I'm much quicker than you and Toad. I shall win all the races I go in for.'

'But that wouldn't be fair,' Cat told her. 'You're not a schoolgirl.'

'Don't you be too sure,' said Witch mysteriously.

Mr Mib drove up to the building on Saturday at ten o'clock. He was pleased to see Cosy there with a basket.

'Hello, Mr Mib,' said Cosy. 'I've brought us a little snack for the journey. It *will* be a nice day out.'

'I do hope so,' said Mr Mib, as Witch came out of the building.

'Hello, Cosy,' said Witch. 'Oh good. You've brought some food. I'm starving. Shall we have something now?'

'Perhaps we should start the journey and have a snack later on,' suggested Mr Mib.

'All right. I'll sit by you and tell you where to go. First I must put my broomstick in the boot. I never go away without it,' Witch told Mr Mib.

He drove the old car steadily, then stopped for an early lunch. As soon as Cosy uncovered her basket, Cat and Toad came out from Witch's bag.

'Gracious heavens! You two as well as

two witches!' exclaimed Mr Mib.

'You're very lucky to have us all,' said Witch. 'Nice full rolls and lovely chocolate cake, Cosy. I shall need a big piece to build up my strength.'

11

'Whatever for?' asked Mr Mib.

'You'll see,' said Witch.

'Oh Witch, what are you up to?' Cosy asked, giggling.

They all found out when Mr Mib drove into the school's car park.

'Good; we're almost the first people here,' said Witch.

Mr Mib turned to look at her and was astonished. Witch had changed into a schoolgirl, dressed in sports kit.

'I've been training for weeks to join in,' said Witch triumphantly, while Cosy laughed helplessly in the back of the car.

'This is no laughing matter,' said Mr Mib. 'You can't drag me here to watch Sports, then suddenly say you're going to take part. You can't just walk in. It's for the boys and girls here at the school.'

'But I'm one of the girls, don't you see. And you'll be my father.'

'Me!' Mr Mib was horrified. 'How could you be my daughter?'

'Just for today,' Witch said. 'I wouldn't want you every day for a father, in case you started bossing me around.'

'Me. Boss you! I wish I could,' said poor Mr Mib.

'And Cosy, you'll be my mother,' Witch went on.

'Oh dear; I'd be no good at that. I never

could stop you doing things when we were at school,' said Cosy.

'And you're not going to now,' added Witch. 'Let's go and see if the Sports are starting.' She hurried on to the playing field with Mr Mib, Cosy, Cat and Toad trailing behind.

Already a lot of children and their parents had arrived. Witch settled in the shade of a tree and began to look at the programme of events. 'A lot of races for me to enter,' she said.

'But Witch,' Mr Mib began to protest.

'Now you just sit here quietly, and clap when I win,' Witch told him.

A teacher with a megaphone announced: 'Please get ready for the first race. A hundred metres.'

Boys and girls went over to the starting post, followed by Witch.

'Listen carefully,' said the teacher. 'I shall say: "On your marks. Get set," then blow my whistle, to start the race. You must not move till you hear the whistle.'

As she spoke there was a loud whistle from near Mr Mib. He was as surprised as everyone else. But luckily only he and Cosy could see Cat blowing a whistle he had found in Witch's bag.

'Cat, stop that at once,' said Mr Mib; 'or I'll put you straight back in the car.'

Cat ran away, saying: 'I was only trying it out, you miserable old spoil-sport!'

'Never mind,' said Cosy. 'He won't do that again.'

'No fooling about, please, children,' said the teacher sternly. 'Now we're all ready. On your marks, get set.' And she blew the whistle loudly.

The children began their race and Witch ran behind them. But it was obvious that she hated being last, so, before anyone reached the winning tape, she waved her hand, and the tape blew up into a tree.

The teacher said: 'Oh dear. Hold it tightly please, children. We'll have to run that race all over again.'

The next time Witch just came in first, but hurried away before a teacher could take her name as winner.

'Odd looking girl,' he said. 'I don't think I know her name. We'll find out later. Reminds me of a terrible girl we once had here; Luola Sprunt she was called. The naughtiest girl I ever knew. Oh well, it's the skipping race next.'

All the skipping ropes were placed

neatly at the starting post. The children laughed when a black cat suddenly ran along the row of ropes. But they didn't laugh when the race began. All the ropes tangled up like snakes. They had knots in them which the girls couldn't straighten out. Only one girl went skipping down the track with her rope swirling over and over as she skipped.

'Lovely skipping,' said Cosy.

'Horrid cheating,' said Mr Mib. 'And to think I'm supposed to be her father. You really must do something to stop her, Cosy.'

'Never mind. She hasn't given her name in to the teachers for winning the race,' said Cosy.

'I should think not,' said Mr Mib, as the skipping race was done again by puzzled girls and cross teachers.

'Who *is* that girl? She seems to have vanished,' said a teacher at the winning post.

'Some child messing about. I shall catch her next time, I'm sure.'

Witch hurried over to Mr Mib and said: 'Come on, Cosy; I need you to be my partner in the three-legged race.'

'But I don't want . . .'

Witch took no notice, and pulled Cosy near to the starting post, then tied their ankles together with a scarf. As soon as the race began Witch said: 'Start now.

Run with me. Left right. Left right. Keep in time.'

Poor Cosy, with her short legs, could not take long strides like Witch. Cosy was puffing, and so out of breath that she

could not speak as she stumbled along, dragged by Witch. The boys and girls were laughing at the odd pair, but Witch shouted angrily, 'Oh, you're hopeless, Cosy!'

Quickly undoing the scarf by magic, Witch hitched Cosy up until she was carrying her under her arm, so that she could run faster. Cosy struggled and kicked, chanting strange words. She was

trying to make enough magic to wriggle out of Witch's clutches. Some wings started sprouting out of her shoulders. With one last kick, Cosy floated upwards, flapping her wings.

Children were pointing and laughing, and a boy shouted: 'Look at her! She's changed into a big bird.' But Cosy only managed to fly over the crowd and back to the tree before her wings shrank to nothing.

Witch dodged a teacher trying to catch her, and stamped back to Mr Mib in a rage.

'Witch, you are behaving very badly,' said Mr Mib.

'*I'm* racing marvellously. We were winning, but Cosy wouldn't join in properly. She was cheating, trying to fly, instead of running like me. It's your turn now. Come on. Fathers' race,' said Witch.

'Certainly not,' said Mr Mib. 'I haven't raced for years.'

'If you don't, I'll make a terrible fuss. It's easy, just jumping in a sack. I'll help you,' said Witch, pulling him along to the starting post.

'That would make things much worse,' Mr Mib declared, feeling silly, lining up with all the real fathers.

'You just get into the sack and hold it up round you, then jump!' said a teacher brightly. 'We've made it a short track, to help you.'

'And that's *enough* help,' said Mr Mib, turning to Witch. But she had vanished.

When the race started, all the fathers tried to jump in big jumps, but often they over-balanced and rolled over. Cat was stepping round the fallen fathers, sniffing at them and waving her tail in their faces, which slowed them up maddeningly. Mr Mib was so nervous that he did a little shuffle inside his sack all down the track, right to the winning tape.

'Well done, sir,' a teacher called to him. 'May I have your name, please?'

'It's Mib. No, I mean I'd rather not say, if you don't mind,' Mr Mib mumbled, and hurried back to Cosy under the tree.

'Splendid,' she said. 'Would you like an extra biscuit?'

'I need one after that,' said Mr Mib. 'The things Witch leads me into!'

'She always led me into trouble when we were . . . Oh look at her now!'

'Whatever next?' asked Mr Mib.

Two teams were getting ready for a tug-of-war. Witch was watching closely as the boys and girls twisted the rope round the last person in each team.

'This contest is just for fun,' said the teacher with the megaphone. 'By special request, we are having girls versus boys.'

The parents and children clapped and laughed, but Witch looked cross.

'I suppose she thought she could join in and get the girls to win with her extra pull,' said Mr Mib. 'Cheating again.'

'I call it more magic than cheating,' said Cosy. 'I hope the girls do win.'

'The boys might be stronger,' Mr Mib told her.

The teacher was explaining that one team had to pull the other over a central point. They would have three tries.

The heaving started, and the boys pulled the girls over to their side.

'Come on, girls,' Witch called out. 'You can do better than that.' She went near to the boys' team, and from her pocket something small leapt out, so quickly that no one noticed.

During the second tug the boys' team began to loose hold, and give way to the girls. First one boy then another let go with a hand to scratch at his neck.

The parents and children shouted as the girls pulled the boys over their way.

Witch began to smile, and by the time the girls had pulled the boys over for a second time she was laughing out loud.

'I don't know. This is the strangest Sports I've ever run,' said the teacher. 'Something was putting those boys off, but I couldn't see what.'

Witch was very pleased with herself, and said: 'The next race is an obstacle race, a very good one for me to win.'

Six people were waiting at the starting post as the race was laid out. Witch watched it all, then set off with them for a row of buckets of water. Each child had to sit down, take off his shoes and socks, dip his feet in the water, dry them, then put on his shoes and socks again.

Toad jumped out of Witch's pocket into the water, and a girl ran away, screaming: 'There's a huge toad in my bucket!'

Witch took her place, only pretended to wet her feet, and took Toad back into her pocket. Then she put her socks and shoes on quickly, and ran on to a big barrel, open at both ends. Witch crawled through in a flash, but the girl following her screamed: 'I'm not going through that! There's a furry creature inside the barrel.'

'We know who that is,' said Mr Mib

grimly to Cosy. 'Go and chase him out.'

Witch went on, laughing, and was rather cross when Cosy chased Cat out of the barrel. She picked up one ball and threw it into a basket, then started throwing the others about, juggling them in the air, till Cosy came panting along and said: 'You shouldn't touch those balls. They're for the others in the race.'

Witch rushed away to the next obstacle, a pile of clothes. She started dressing up in a long skirt, a big hat and sunglasses. Then she put up an umbrella and ran away from two boys who were struggling to catch her up. Next Witch jumped over a log, and walked along a

ladder placed flat on the ground. She looked behind to see who was following her and fell over. By now she was furious, so she tried to trip up the boys with her umbrella. They managed to get past her and ran to the winning tape. Witch ran with them, past a teacher who said:

'My eyes must be playing tricks. I'm sure there was an extra girl in that race sometimes, but there are only three finishing off now.'

Witch was in a tantrum by the time she reached Mr Mib and Cosy again. 'You spoilt that last race too,' she told Cosy. 'Still at least I'll be getting my prize in a minute, before we have tea.'

'But you haven't won a prize,' said Mr Mib.

'I don't see why not,' said Witch. And when they all gathered round the table for the prize giving, Witch was on the front row.

The Headmaster said: 'Thank you very much to the teachers who have worked so hard to prepare the Sports, and to the parents for coming to support us. The boys and girls have raced well. And we must remember that it is not only winning that counts, but taking part. So I don't want to see any races spoilt by unsporting behaviour. Now for the prizes.'

Witch looked worried as the cups and medals were given out. When the Headmaster picked up the last cup it suddenly seemed to fly out of his hands.

Everyone gasped as Witch rose into the air on her broomstick, clutching the cup.

'Stop thief!' shouted the Headmaster. 'Catch that girl.'

But nobody could. They stood watching helplessly.

Mr Mib was horrified. 'What a disgrace! Do something, Cosy. Where can she have gone?'

'I don't know. Probably to hide it,' answered Cosy. 'We used to hide things when we were here together.'

'Then go and find her and get it back,' said Mr Mib. 'Can't you fly after her or something?'

'That's too hard magic for me twice in an afternoon,' said Cosy, but she hurried off after Witch, running as fast as she could.

Mr Mib waited anxiously. One of the teachers came up and asked: 'Please have you seen that girl who was under this tree, sir?'

'I haven't seen her for some time,' said Mr Mib rather gratefully. All he wanted was to return the cup and go home.

Cosy did find Witch, hiding in the back of Mr Mib's car.

'You've got to give the cup back, Witch,' she said.

'Shan't,' said Witch. 'It's mine now. Did you see that fantastic flying? Much higher than your flopping about.'

'I was quite pleased with my wings, as I've never managed to fly before,' said Cosy modestly.

'Oh, I could teach you to grow much bigger wings than that. And they wouldn't shrivel away in two minutes either,' said Witch.

'Perhaps we could have a try later,' said Cosy, 'but that cup is due back now. Someone else won it, not you.'

'Only because I didn't give my name to the teachers all the times I came in first.'

'But you're not a schoolgirl any more, don't you see? You're a grown-up witch. Can't you think of a clever way to give it back to them?' Cosy asked.

Witch smiled to herself and began to grow slowly. Cosy realised that she was with a policewoman.

'Now that I've found the stolen cup,' said Policewoman Witch, 'I must return it to the Headmaster.'

She strode back to the field, and gave the cup to the Headmaster. 'I didn't catch the girl, but I have rescued the cup.'

'Wonderful,' exclaimed the Headmaster, and gave the cup to the boy who had won it, while everyone clapped loudly.

Witch stayed as Policewoman Witch all through tea, but on the way home she changed back to herself. 'I'm quite worn out with racing,' she said. 'It's such hard work being a Sporty Witch.'